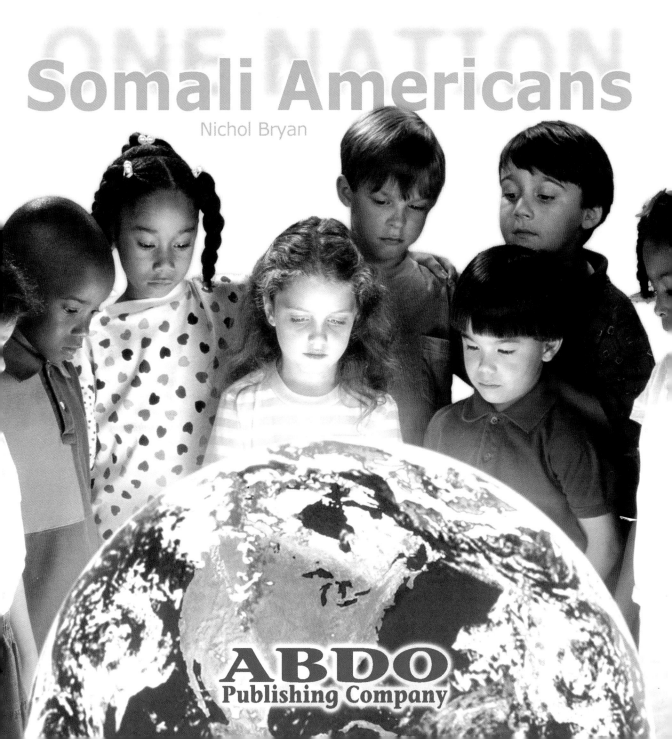

Somali Americans

ONE NATION

Nichol Bryan

ABDO
Publishing Company

visit us at
www.abdopub.com

Published by ABDO Publishing Company, 4940 Viking Drive, Edina, Minnesota 55435.
Copyright © 2004 by Abdo Consulting Group, Inc. International copyrights reserved in all
countries. No part of this book may be reproduced in any form without written permission from
the publisher.

Printed in the United States.

Cover Photo: Portland Press Herald/Maine Sunday Telegram
Interior Photos: AP/Wide World pp. 7, 12, 15, 16, 20, 21, 22, 23, 29; Corbis pp. 1, 2-3, 9, 10, 25,
    27, 30-31; Getty Images pp. 11, 28; Portland Press Herald/Maine Sunday Telegram pp. 5, 19

Editors: Kate A. Conley, Jennifer R. Krueger, Kristin Van Cleaf
Art Direction & Maps: Neil Klinepier

All of the U.S. population statistics in the One Nation series are taken from the 2000 Census.

Library of Congress Cataloging-in-Publication Data

Bryan, Nichol, 1958-
    Somali Americans / Nichol Bryan.
        p. cm. -- (One nation)
    Summary: Provides an overview of the life and culture of Somali Americans and presents
some information on the history of Somalia.
    Includes bibliographical references and index.
    ISBN 1-57765-989-9
    1. Somali Americans--Juvenile literature. [1. Somali Americans. 2. Refugees. 3.
Immigrants.] I. Title.

E184.S67B78 2003
973'.0496773--dc21

                                                                        2002043631

Contents

Somali Americans

America is a land of **immigrants**. For hundreds of years, America has been a place of hope and opportunity for millions of people who have left their homes behind. In fact, most Americans have ancestors who have made this journey to America.

Some of these immigrants fled their country to practice their religion. Some left to make a better living for their family. Most came for the safety, freedom, or opportunity that did not exist in their home country. Somali immigrants moved to America for many of these reasons.

Somali immigrants came from an ancient land of **nomads** and poets. But, their homeland also has a history of **civil war** and **famine**. Today, many Somalis have immigrated to the United States in search of a better life for themselves and their families.

Opposite page: A Somali-American girl plays basketball with her friend in Lewiston, Maine.

Somalia's Past

Somalia is in eastern Africa, on what is called the Horn of Africa. It points eastward into the Indian Ocean. Somalia is about the size of the state of Texas. The land includes coastline, flatland, and some rolling hills and mountains.

Somalia lies on the **equator**, so it is very warm. Rainfall is scarce in many parts, and life can be hard for the people because of this. Most Somalis are either farmers or **nomads**. It is hard to grow food and to feed animals when there is no rain. But, life is even harder for Somalis because of the political situation in their country. To understand this situation, it is necessary to look at a bit of Somalian history.

Somalis have lived on the Horn of Africa for about 2,000 years. Early in their history, Somalis were nomads. They moved south from the coast of the Gulf of Aden in the A.D. 800s or 900s. However, the interior of Somalia remained a mystery to outsiders

A Somali boy stands in the wind on a hill near Mogadishu.

until the 1800s. At this time, Britain, Italy, and France competed for Somalian land.

By the late 1800s, most of Somalia was under foreign rule. The British ruled northern Somalia, the French ruled northwestern Somalia, and the Italians ruled parts of southern Somalia. Somalia gained its independence from Italy and Britain in 1960. After this, the country was ruled by a group of people from both northern and southern Somalia.

In 1967, Abdi Rashid Ali Shermarke was elected president. Just two years later, however, he was **assassinated**. That same year, Maxamed Siyaad Barre took over the government. He had been the commander of the Somalian army. Siyaad Barre made Somalia a **socialist** state.

During Siyaad Barre's rule, France granted independence to the people in its Somalian territory in 1977. This area became Djibouti, a country north of Somalia. While Siyaad Barre ruled, Somalia also fought with Ethiopia over land. Ethiopia and Somalia signed a peace agreement in 1988. Some Somalis did not like the agreement, though, and they wanted Siyaad Barre out of power.

Many different Somali groups forced Siyaad Barre out of office in 1991. After this, there was no one to rule the country. The different clans fought among themselves for control of Somalia.

At this time, Somalia was a terrible place to live. The fighting kept Somalis from carrying on with their normal lives. Farmers couldn't grow food, and **nomads** couldn't herd their animals. The fighting also prevented people from receiving emergency food supplies sent from other countries. All these events caused a **famine** that killed thousands.

A Somali soldier holds a picture of Maxamed Siyaad Barre after Siyaad Barre was overthrown in 1991.

The fighting and the **famine** hurt children the most. Many died at birth. Others died of disease or starvation in their early years. Still others were almost constantly ill. Many Somalis recognized the importance of forming a government and stopping the fighting.

An American soldier laughs with young Somalis.

The United Nations (UN) and the United States tried to help in 1993. But, many Somalis, Americans, and UN workers died in the fighting. Mogadishu, Somalia's capital, became a place where only the fighters had food. No one was safe.

In 2000, Somalis created the Transitional National Government (TNG), a temporary government for Somalia. They also elected a president for the government, Abdiqassim Salad Hassan. The TNG was given three years to create a permanent, stable Somalian government. Until this happens, however, uncertainty is everywhere.

Today, Somalia remains a dangerous place. The U.S. government warns Americans not to visit because of kidnappings and murders there. The instability has hurt the Somalian **economy**. The average Somali earns less than $600 a year. As a result, Somalis continue to leave their war-torn land.

Supporters of Abdiqassim Salad Hassan celebrate after his election.

Fleeing Somalia

Millions of Somalis were forced to leave their homes when the fighting started. Sometimes they left so quickly they had only the clothing they wore. Some of these people remained in Somalia, but they had no homes. Many of them became **refugees**.

The first refugees found themselves in nearby countries such as Ethiopia, Kenya, and Yemen. They often had to live in crude **camps**. There was not always enough to eat, and water was scarce. In these conditions, it was hard to stay healthy.

Although immigrating is not easy, many Somali Americans say it was worth the hardship.

The UN, private groups, and religious groups came to the rescue of some of these desperate people. They asked the governments of other countries to accept the Somali **refugees**. They often arranged for Somalis to come to the United States.

The Journey from Somalia to the United States

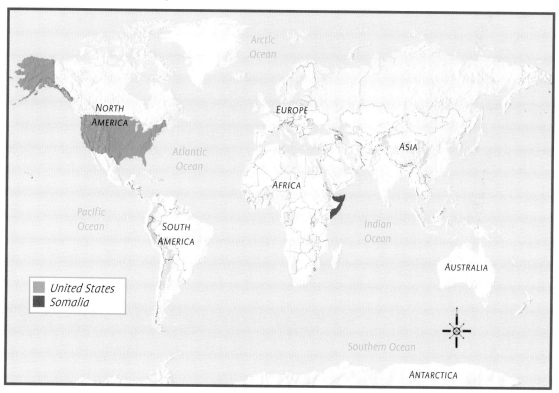

Challenges

Before the 1990s, few Somalis lived in the United States. They knew that becoming U.S. citizens would be a long and difficult process. They also knew that they could be the targets of **discrimination** in their new homes. They wondered how their Muslim faith would be viewed in a mostly Christian country.

Their fears were balanced by their hopes. America had always been a land of opportunity. Somalis believed that by working hard, they could enjoy life in the United States. If nothing else, their new home would be safer than Somalia.

The first Somalis who came to the United States found life very hard. Everything was so different! Fortunately, members of their new communities helped them find homes and jobs. Soon, the first Somali Americans were settled and able to help new arrivals.

However, many Somalis seeking **asylum** had no family members or friends to assist them. For most Somali **immigrants**, arriving in America is a difficult experience. Some people even accuse the

Somali immigrants take the oath of citizenship.

Immigration and Naturalization Service of placing Somali **refugees** in jail or prison. These people say that Somalis are moved from one place to another, making it hard to find legal help.

Other issues trouble Somali Americans. Some Somalis who had been living and working in the United States were sent back to Somalia. Some were **deported** because they had committed crimes in the United States. Many Somalis say these deportations are not right. They say Somalis who return to their native land risk being killed.

Despite these troubles, coming to America has been worth the effort for most Somalis. They enjoy life in cities such as Atlanta, Columbus, San Diego, Seattle, Washington, D.C., and Minneapolis. In fact, Minneapolis may have as many as 50,000 Somali Americans. That's more than any other U.S. city!

Somali Americans have adjusted to a very different life, learned a new language, and learned how American society works. Some take classes in order to learn English. Others have gone on

In many communities, Somalis struggle to get along with their new neighbors.

to start businesses that serve the Somali community. But, even as they work to **assimilate** into American **culture**, others often single them out.

For example, some Americans are suspicious of Muslims. That's because on September 11, 2001, a small group of Muslims committed **terrorist** attacks against the United States. Most Muslims, however, are peaceful. Somalis work to educate others about their faith and culture, hoping this will lessen the fear and suspicion they often face.

Somali-American Communities

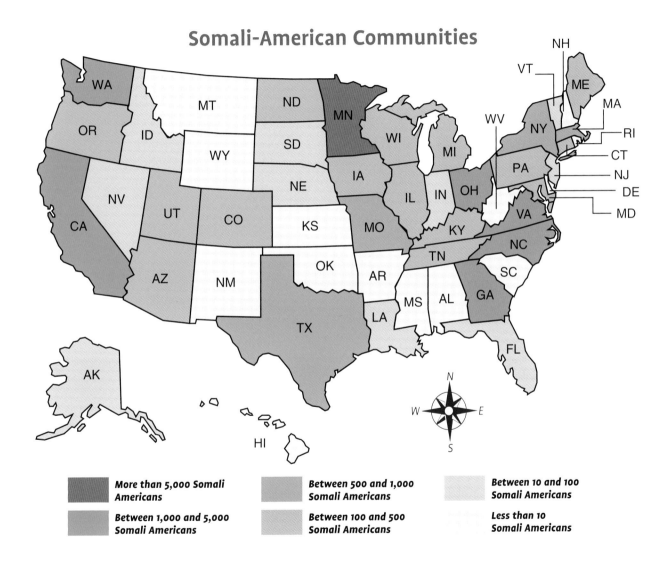

Legend:
- More than 5,000 Somali Americans
- Between 1,000 and 5,000 Somali Americans
- Between 500 and 1,000 Somali Americans
- Between 100 and 500 Somali Americans
- Between 10 and 100 Somali Americans
- Less than 10 Somali Americans

Becoming a Citizen

Somalis and other **immigrants** who come to the United States take the same path to citizenship. Immigrants become citizens in a process called naturalization. A government agency called the Immigration and Naturalization Service (INS) oversees this process.

The Path to Citizenship

Applying for Citizenship

The first step in becoming a citizen is filling out a form. It is called the Application for Naturalization. On the application, immigrants provide information about their past. Immigrants send the application to the INS.

Providing Information

Besides the application, immigrants must provide the INS with other items. They may include documents such as marriage licenses or old tax returns. Immigrants must also provide photographs and fingerprints. They are used for identification. The fingerprints are also used to check whether immigrants have committed crimes in the past.

The Interview

Next, an INS officer interviews each immigrant to discuss his or her application and background. In addition, the INS officer tests the immigrant's ability to speak, read, and write in English. The officer also tests the immigrant's knowledge of American civics.

The Oath

Immigrants approved for citizenship must take the Oath of Allegiance. Once immigrants take this oath, they are citizens. During the oath, immigrants promise to renounce loyalty to their native country, to support the U.S. Constitution, and to serve and defend the United States when needed.

Sample Questions from the Civics Test

How many stars are there on our flag?

What is the capital of the state you live in?

Why did the pilgrims come to America?

How many senators are there in Congress?

Who said, "Give me liberty or give me death"?

What are the first 10 amendments to the Constitution called?

In what month do we vote for the president?

Why Become a Citizen?

Why would an immigrant want to become a U.S. citizen? There are many reasons. Perhaps the biggest reason is that the U.S. Constitution grants many rights to its citizens. One of the most important is the right to vote.

U.S. Department of Justice
Immigration and Naturalization Service

Print clearly or type your answers using CAPITAL letters. Failure to print clearly may delay your application. Use bla[

Application fo

Part 1. Your Name *(The Person Applying for Naturalization)*

A. Your current legal name.

Family Name *(Last Name)*

Write your INS "A"- nu
A _ _ _ _ _ _ _

Given Name *(First Name)*

Full Middle Name *(If applicable)*

FOR INS US

Bar Code

B. Your name exactly as it appears on your Permanent Resident Card.

Family Name *(Last Name)*

Given Name *(First Name)*

Full Middle Name *(If applicable)*

C. If you have ever used other names, provide them below.

Family Name *(Last Name)*

Given Name *(First Name)*

Middle Name

Life in America

In each community where they settle, Somali Americans bring unique **customs** and a new **culture**. This culture includes views on family, religion, food, and language.

Family

Somali families include children, parents, and grandparents, just like most American families. Somalis also believe in clans, families that include hundreds of people related by birth and marriage. Most Somalis are very loyal to their clan. But in Somalia, several large clans continue to fight among themselves.

A Somali-American family

20

Somalis also feel that the immediate family is very important. Women sometimes marry at age 14 or 15 to start their own families. Some marry a person picked by their parents. Traditionally, fathers work outside the home. Traditional Somali mothers usually do work that lets them stay in the home.

Many Somali-American women are working outside of the home in shops like this one.

The role of women in Somali-American communities is changing. More women are working outside of the home. However, some women blend the old with the new by creating and wearing Somalian clothing. For example, many Somali-American women have jobs, but also wear a long dress called a *hijab*.

A Worldwide Faith

Most Somali Americans are Sunni Muslims, followers of a branch of Islam. Islam has been a major faith in Africa, the Middle East, and Asia for more than 1,000 years. A Muslim prophet named Muhammad preached submission to one god, Allah. The teachings of Allah are recorded in a book called the Koran.

A Somali-American man reads from the Koran.

Many of the day-to-day habits of Somalis come from the teachings of Islam. For instance, the Koran encourages modesty. So, Somali men and women avoid tight-fitting clothing, and women wear head coverings. Like other Muslims, Somalis also find guidance in the Five Pillars of Islam, a set of acts they must follow.

The Importance of Ramadan

An important part of Islam is the holy month of Ramadan. Ramadan is the ninth month of the Islamic calendar. It is said to be the month the prophet Muhammad first received the teachings from Allah that make up the Koran.

Muslims observe Ramadan in special ways. For example, they fast from sunrise to sunset for the entire month. Muslims see fasting as a way to purify and renew themselves. The end of Ramadan is observed with a festival called Eid al-Fitr that includes eating and giving gifts. The celebration lasts for three days.

A Somali American celebrates at an antidiscrimination rally.

Somalian Food

Islam also teaches about diet. Because of their beliefs, most Somalis avoid eating pork. They also stay away from alcohol. Somalis eat a small breakfast and dinner, and a big lunch.

Meats such as goat, beef, and lamb are an important part of all Somalian meals. In addition, because of their contact with Italians in Somalia, Somalis also like spaghetti! Some of their favorite foods, however, can't be found in the United States. For example, Somalis drink camel milk in Somalia, but that is very hard to find in America.

An Ancient Language

People in Somalia mostly speak Somali and Arabic. Somali is a rich language that has been spoken for centuries. However, this language had no written form until 1972. Then people developed a written form of Somali that uses the Latin alphabet, just like English.

Because Somalia was once under Italian and British rule, Italian and English are also sometimes spoken in Somalia. So, some Somali **immigrants** may know English before they reach the United

States. While most Somali Americans learn English in the United States, many still speak Somali in their homes.

Somalis say that poetry and Islam are the two pillars of their **culture**. In Somalia, poetry competitions were very important events. Poets helped people remember history, share news, and comment on the government.

Although the role of poetry is less noticeable in modern-day Somalia, it is still an important part of Somali culture. In the United States, Somalis still strongly value their language traditions.

A part of the Koran written in Arabic

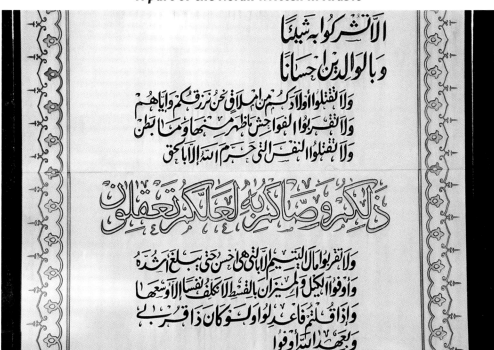

Growing Fame

Most Somali Americans did not come to the United States until the early 1990s. Yet, several Somalis are well known in America and around the world.

One well-known Somali American is Iman, a fashion model. Iman was born in Mogadishu, Somalia, in 1955. She traveled to Kenya to attend college. While she was there, a fashion photographer discovered her, and she started her modeling career.

Iman has traveled all over the world for her work. Along the way, she has used the five languages she was taught as a child! Now, Iman lives in New York with her husband. She owns two beauty companies and also works for several charities. Iman has become an important role model for Somali women who are trying to find their place in American life.

Opposite page: Iman

Abdi Bile

Distance runner Abdi Bile is another Somali American who has accomplished much in the United States. He was born in Las Anod, Somalia. He attended college in the United States and competed in the Olympics several times. In 1987, he was the 1500m world champion. He continues to give talks with advice for runners, and he serves as a role model for all aspiring athletes.

Ali Khalif Galaydh is also well known in Somalia and in America. In fact, he was Somalia's **prime minister** from 2000 to 2001. Galaydh moved to the United States 18 years ago. He returned to Somalia when he was elected to office. Now, he's back in Minnesota with his family and teaches at the University of Minnesota.

Ali Khalif Galaydh

Even these famous Somali Americans have had to cope with the challenges facing most Somali **immigrants**. Somalis have left a dangerous land for unfamiliar surroundings. But, they still approach life with hope and determination. As they make their homes in the United States, Somalis are sure to make an even bigger impact on American **culture**.

Glossary

assassinate - to murder a very important person, usually for political reasons.

assimilate - to become a comfortable part of a new culture or society.

asylum - protection in another country from persecution in a person's home country.

camp - a place where civilians live temporarily, sometimes against their will.

civil war - a war between groups in the same country.

culture - the customs, arts, and tools of a nation or people at a certain time.

customs - the habits of a group that are passed on through generations.

deport - to force someone who is not a citizen to leave the country.

discrimination - unfair treatment based on factors such as a person's race, religion, or gender.

economy - the way a nation uses its money, goods, and natural resources.

equator - an imaginary circle around the middle of Earth.

famine - a severe scarcity of food.

immigration - entry into another country to live. A person who immigrates is called an immigrant.

nomad - a member of a tribe that moves from place to place.

prime minister - the highest-ranked member of some governments.

refugee - a person who flees to another country for safety and protection.

socialism - a kind of economy. The government or the citizens control the production and distribution of goods.

terrorist - a person who uses violence to threaten people or governments.

Saying It

Abdi Bile - AHB-dee BIHL-leh
Abdiqassim Salad Hassan - ab-dee-KA-seem SAH-lad HAH-sahn
Abdi Rashid Ali Shermarke - AHB-dee-rah-SHEED ah-LEE shar-mah-AHR-keh
Ali Khalif Galaydh - ah-LEE ha-LEEF gah-LAYD
hijab - hih-JAB
Iman - EE-mahn
Maxamed Siyaad Barre - mah-HAH-mehd see-YAHD bar-REH

Web Sites

To learn more about Somali Americans, visit ABDO Publishing Company on the World Wide Web at **www.abdopub.com**. Web sites about Somali Americans are featured on our Book Links page. These links are routinely monitored and updated to provide the most current information available.

Index